Shirley Temple Dolls and Collectibles

Second Series

by

Patricia R. Smith

Cover: Bluebird Doll - Meisinger Collection
Photo by Joe V. Ragusa

Published by COLLECTOR BOOKS
P.O. Box 3009
Paducah, Kentucky 42001

Additional copies of this book may be ordered from:

COLLECTOR BOOKS
P.O. Box 3009
Paducah, Kentucky 42001

@ $17.95 Add $.50 postage for the first book &
$.20 for each additional book.

Copyright: Patricia R. Smith, Bill Schroeder, 1979
ISBN: 0-89145-113-7

Printed by PURCHASE PRINTERS, Paducah, Kentucky

Dedication

The adoration felt by millions for the little girl, Shirley Temple, can be defined clinically, logically and even through physiology, as one thing . . . love. The love is that of a father and mother for their child, an aunt for her niece, a grand-mother for her grand-daughter, and even the love of a child projected towards her yet unborn. Through the movie screen little Shirley Temple was able to reflect the love each saw in their own loved ones that were, or were yet to come. Therefore this book is dedicated to two in the lives of others: Judy Meisinger, the "Shirley" in her parents lives, and to Bonnie Jean Gibson, the "Shirley" in my own life. It is our sincerest desire that, as adults, these two "Shirleys" offer life and humanity as much as the real Shirley Temple Black.

Credits

Once again, as with Volume 1, my deepest thanks must go to Marge Meisinger, for without her this Volume would have been much more difficult to do. Marge Meisinger stands for what collecting is all about . . . sharing, and caring!

Marge Meisinger - photos by Mike Scheer and Dwight Smith
Alma Carmichael - photos by Dwight Smith
Millie Busch
Rita Dubas - photos by John DeLuca

Eloise Godfrey
Maxine Heitt - photos by Dwight Smith
Phyllis Houston
Thelma Kimble
Ruth Lane
Carol Meisinger - photos by Mike Scheer
Loretta Zablotny

and to Mollye Goldman, my very special friend, whose life revolved around the little girl in the movies even more closely than most.

This portrait shot is of the Shirley Temple Baby. Composition and has flirty eyes. Note how low the dimples are. Courtesy Alma Carmichael.

Contents

Because the content page is so complete, there will be no index included.

Why Do I Collect?

by Marge Meisinger

Authors note: We have received hundreds of letters asking how in the world Marge Meisinger could have built the collection she has. Marge, herself, is asked this same question, over and over, so we asked her to write the following for all of us.

To a collector, finding something "new" to add to their collection is very exciting, and Shirley Temple collectors are no different. I am constantly finding "new" items, but this is no surprise, since no little girl ever had so many items with her name or likeness on them. Many of the items were authorized, but there is no mistaking the little blonde with the curls, dimples and smile, so whether her name is on the item or not, everyone knows it's "Shirley Temple". It's the things that also have her name that are the most sought after, as they are considered authentic.

When asked how long I have been collecting, I usually reply, "Since about 1964". Before that I saved a lot of Shirley items, including books, tablets, etc. that I'd had in the 1930's; but after 1964, I went searching and came up with hundreds of items I didn't even know existed. Who would think to look in cigar band collectors wares for one picturing Shirley, yet they are there. There are several decks of cards with different pictures of Shirley Temple, Sweet Pea Flower seeds named for Shirley in 1936, hundreds of magazines featuring her (I have over 200 with her on the covers, alone), jewelry such as charm bracelets, pins, necklaces, etc. (these are some of the favorite items in my collection), and a Shirley Temple Police Badge (Shirley gave these to people at the studio and to visiting dignitaries, such as J. Edgar Hoover, Henry Morganthau, etc.). There are even hundreds of postcards, cigarette cards and candy cards, etc., that were made in England, Holland, Germany and other countries.

In 1959, the 35" Shirley Temple appeared in the toy stores, and I visited one store several times to look at the doll before buying it. I wanted the doll

for my younger daughter, Judy, but with 6 children, it seemed like a lot of money. I knew I would regret it if I didn't buy the doll though, so Judy got her doll for Christmas and still has it, original box and all.

It was very rewarding when Patricia Smith asked me if she could feature my collection in a book. Being able to share a collection justifies it, I think, whether you just show it to interested collectors, or share information. The book was released November 1977, and is very beautiful and informative. There are still many things to learn in the field of Shirley Temple collecting, and through the Shirley Temple Club, we are able to share information. The President of the Club is in Anchorage, Alaska and her address is: Jackie Musgrave, P.O. Box 524, Anchorage, AL 99570. If you are interested in everything of Shirley, right up to the present time, by all means join this club.

When people see, or hear of our collection, the questions we are most often asked are, "How long have you been collecting?", and "What started you collecting?" As I have said, I saved a lot of things from the 1930's, but really started looking and collecting memorabilia about 1964. In the 1950's I bought a Shirley Temple doll to keep, and also the 35" Shirley for Judy. I still think that 35" doll is the most beautiful Shirley there is. I also bought song albums, records, etc. and several "Cinderella" Shirley Temple dresses for my two daughters, JeJe and Judy, jewelry and several other Shirley items.

Early in the 1960's I heard about Ione Wollenzein's Shirley Temple Museum in Waukesha, Wisconsin (no longer operating) and I wrote to her. I visited several times and thought her museum was the most beautiful collection I'd ever seen. I then heard about the Shirley Temple Club organized by Loraine Burdick and I was off with a flying start. It was easy collecting then, as I was the only one in this area and soon had quite a few correspondents, all interested in collecting

Shirley Temple items. I introduced several collectors to the club, met some such as our very dearest friends, Barb and LeRoy Taylor, through "want ads" in the pages of a magazine. There are also a lot of overseas collectors I trade with, so I have acquired a number of beautiful Shirley articles from many foreign countries. Notably among these foreign items are the beautiful film magazines and annuals from England, also from England are the postcards, cigarette cards, etc. Many of these same items came from Holland, Spain, Germany and Italy.

I wonder if Shirley Temple Black can ever really understand the sunshine she brought into so many lives. I lived on a farm in the 1930's and many Saturdays, my brother and I went to the movies. I remember the first Shirley Temple movie I saw, "Bright Eyes", and after that I saved everything I found in newspapers and magazines. The Chicago Daily News often had full pages of pictures of Shirley, and almost every magazine featured her at sometime or other. Photos of her were given away at groceries, theaters, etc., and the movie magazines! I thought they were absolutely gorgeous. It was truly the Golden Age of Hollywood and never since that time have movie magazines been as beautiful.

So many wonderful people have helped with my collection. Many of them had dolls they wanted a collector to have, my children, relatives and friends watched for Shirley items for me. One of my daughters-in-law, Carol, found a mint Shirley doll in the original box, just last year in Iowa. Ten years ago, my son David, kept asking a shop owner in Chicago for the poster of Shirley Temple on his wall, it was the only one he had, but David finally got it for me.

New items, also many reproductions, continually turn up and there is always the "will-o-the wisp" authentic item to search for. Until I started collecting, I never realized there were so many hundreds of things using Shirley's name and picture, but finding these now is what makes collecting fun. The greatest thing about my collecting is my husband, Earl. His interest and cooperation is priceless and without him, it wouldn't have been possible for me to have the collection.

CHAIRMAN OF THE BOARD   December 15, 1978

Ms. Patricia R. Smith
1522 West 27th Terrace
Independence, Missouri   64052

Dear Ms. Smith:

Mrs. Addie Riley has asked me to answer your letter of Nov. 20th.

Mollye Goldman is a long time friend. For years - since 1928
or 1929 - long before Shirley Temple dolls - Mollye Goldman
was engaged as a contractor to design and manufacture doll
dresses and outfits for us.

Most of the Shirley Temple dolls wore the replicas of the
dresses or costumes Shirley wore in her motion pictures.
They were reduced to doll size.   Mollye made a great many
of them for us.

Ideal Toy Corp. were not her only customers. She had a factory
in Chester, Pa., where she produced doll dresses for the stores
and for other doll manufacturers.

Mollye Goldman was our favorite contractor for doll clothes.
As you say, she was - and is, altho I regret I have not seen
her recently - a delightful, dynamic person who did whatever
she undertook, well.

As we made most of our doll dresses inside our own plant, con-
tracting out never over 40% at most to others because of in-
ability to meet peak demand, Mollye Goldman was engaged to
train our operators.

Her work was under supervision of Miss Mary Maidenbauer, Ideal's
then Vice President of Doll Production, and of course, Mr.
A. M. Katz, my partner, who was head of all manufacturing of
Ideal Toy Corporation.

Cordially

B. F. Michton

A Few Words . . .

A great many magazines, books and articles have been written about Shirley Temple, the child, and any library will fill the desire for knowledge in this area. The same holds true for the adult Shirley, but this has not been included in many collector books.

Shirley's career and first marriage were over and she emerged from this period of her life quietly and deeply sad with only one seemingly point of happiness, her child, Linda Susan Agar (known as Susan). Taking her child and her mother and father, Shirley flew to Hawaii in January of 1950.

While in Hawaii Shirley met Charles Alden Black, who was in Hawaii as assistant to the President of Hawaiian Pineapple. He and Shirley were married on December 16, 1950 at his parents home in Monterey, California. He legally adopted Susan and the Blacks moved into a house in Bel-Air. It was April of 1951 that Charles was recalled to the Navy and sent to Washington D.C. In closing up the Bel-Air house one of the decisions Shirley had to make was what to do with her doll collection, which numbered 740 and was insured for $30,000.00. The doll collection was loaned to the State of California and put on display at the State Exposition Building in Los Angeles.

The Blacks drove towards Washington, but Shirley and Susan had to make a stop over at Tulsa, Oklahoma as Shirley's appendix had to be removed. Eventually they got settled in an apartment on Wyoming Ave. in Washington D.C.

Charles Alden Black, Jr. was born April 28, 1952 by Caesarean section and it was during 1952 that Shirley got a severe case of chicken pox and was quite ill.

The Blacks moved into their own home in Bethesda, Maryland. They gave small dinner parties and attended many, including Embassy dinners, where they met government officials and foreign diplomats and discussed all the issues of the day. All this was a completely new area of interest to Shirley and the Blacks got even more involved after Dwight Eisenhower was elected in 1952.

The Blacks moved back to California after Charles was discharged from the Navy with the end of the Korean War. By May of 1953 he had gone to work for KABC-TV as business manager. It was on April 9, 1954 that Shirley returned to the Santa Monica Hospital where she was born, to give birth to her third child and second daughter, Lori Alden Black. The same nurse who attended Shirley's own birth and that of Linda Susan, was called in at Lori's birth.

In September of 1954, the Blacks moved to Atherton, just twenty-eight miles south of San Francisco, after Charles became the director for the Stanford University Research Institute. Their house was a plain, California style one story home in a very Upper middle class community. The Blacks were very consevative and this home suited them. The house was decorated as Shirley liked it with Oriental furniture mixed with other things that she also liked, such as the carriage lamps from the gates of the Bethesda house. A rock garden, a fountain and even a Buddha statue arose from the patio at the rear of the home, and Shirley planted birds-of-paradise. She was a house wife and did all her own cooking and her only help was a lady to help clean once a week.

The child Shirley Temple would be seen throughout this home with such items as the bookcase in the living room that held the brown leather albums, each with the name of one of her movies imprinted in gold. The albums contained stills and clippings about each of the films. In Lori's room there was a screen with pictures of the child Shirley, Charlie's room had a photo of her as a child and the oldest child, Susan's, room had a great many dolls. Little Lori was given a Shirley Temple doll on her third Christmas. The children were exposed to their mother's childhood, but were not subjected with thoughts of the movies or movie stars.

Shirley was active in groups that helped children, such as the Allied Arts Guild that supported a children's convalescent home, and worked in the national organization for multiple sclerosis after her brother, George, developed this disease. She was a member of the Peninsula Children's Theatre and helped by ushering, painting scenery and served as publicity and hospitality chairman, but was never asked to act. In 1954 both Blacks joined the Sierra Club which is dedicated to the problems of ecology.

In 1957 Charles became the director of corporate relations for the Ampex Corporation, and Shirley finally gave in to doing a television series, although she had turned many down since 1950. The series was to be called the "Shirley Temple's Storybook".

When asked about the Storybook series, Shirley's reply included, "As a child I lived in a storybook world. I was Heidi, Wee Willie Winkie and the Little Princess. Nothing was impossible and it all seemed real."

The "Shirley Temple Storybook" opened and closed with Shirley singing the song "Dreams Are Made For Children". (written by Mack Davis and Jerry Lingstone) and it was the first time Shirley had sung in public since she was eleven.

"Beauty and the Beast" was the opening show of the sixteen show series. Others included "The Legend of Sleepy Hollow" (Starring Shirley), "Rumpelstiltskin", "The Nightingale", "Dick Whittington and His Cat", "Hiawatha", "Charlotte's Web" and the "Son of Aladdin". Shirley also played in the show called "Mother Goose", when she played the part of Polly Put The Kettle On, on a Christmas 1958 show. Susan, Charles and Lori were also on this show and this was their one and only acting debut. The girls did very well, but Charles gave a tight lipped performance.

The Shirley Temple Storybook series ran in 1957 and 1958 and at this same time the Ideal toy company re-issued the Shirley Temple doll. There were a great many different outfits issued for this vinyl doll of the 1950's, but only a few revolved around the series itself. Of the sixteen shows, Shirley only acted in three of them and was Hostess-narrator for the remaining thirteen.

The sponsors for the Shirley Temple Storybook was Hills Brothers Coffee and Sealtest as West and East Coast sponsors and the Breck Hair Products as the nation-wide sponsors. It was shown on NBC. The last Storybook show was taped in March of 1961 and shown later that year.

Shirley Temple appeared on T.V. again in 1963 in the hour long Red Skelton show. She sang "Side by Side" with Red Skelton, and sang "By The Beautiful Sea". In the Freddie the Freeloader sketch, she played a very rich girl. The actual tap-ing of this show was on Shirley's 33rd birthday, April 23, 1963.

In 1965 Shirley again ventured into television and the show was to be taped at her old studio, Twentieth Century Fox. Over the main gate flew a banner, "Welcome Home, Shirley" and there was champagne lunch in the commissary with studio executives and old friends.

The pilot for the projected series to be taped was "Go Fight City Hall" and Shirley played the part of a social worker. It was a half hour pilot and was being made for the American Broadcasting Company (ABC), but they did not buy the series, after seeing the pilot.

Shirley had been active in the Republican Party since the days the Blacks lived in Washington D.C., but it wasn't until the 1960 Presidential election that she became actively involved. She worked as a precinct captain for Richard Nixon against John F. Kennedy and did a thousand other jobs to help the campaign, such as walking door to door, stuffing envelopes, etc. Nixon won the county and state but not the election. Again she was active for Barry Goildwater, but he lost to Lyndon Johnson in 1964. She began accepting fund raising rallies and speaking engagements for the party.

Shirley ran for Congress in 1967 after seeing the Representative J. Arthur Younger (California) would be too ill to run again. Younger had been the 11th Congressional for twelve years and he died in June of that same year. Some of those that advised her to run was George Murphy and Ronald Reagan, both who had been co-stars with her. George Murphy had become Republican Senator, and Reagan was the Governor fo California.

She told a press conference 'Little Shirley Temple is not running for anything, and if someone insists on pinning me with a label make it read Shirley Temple Black, Republican independent'. The thirty-nine year old housewife and ex-movie star faced the battery of cameras like a pro and she demanded to be taken seriously. All she seemed to be asked about was the Vietnam War and not other things that she was deeply feeling about, such as lowering the voting age to 18 and getting the People's Republic of China into the United Nations. She entered the race late and just didn't have the time to make a good campaign.

Her opponent, Democrat Roy Archibald, city counsellor and former Mayor of San Mateo gave his campaign the image "PT-453 versus The Good Ship Lollipop". He had been skipper of a PT boat during World War II just as President Kennedy had been. A popular bumper sticker was "Shirley You Jest" and was seen on both Republican and Democrat cars.

Shirley did not win the seat in Congress, and went on in 1968 to make over two hundred speeches across the country even before Nixon and Agnew were chosen to run. After they were choosen, Shirley visited nine foreign countries on behalf of Nixon. Absentee ballots from abroad went heavily for Nixon-Agnew, who just about didn't make it at home.

Shirley Temple Black, in 1969, was appointed by Nixon to the United States delegate to the United Nations, for the international organization's twenty-fourth General Assembly.

August 20th of 1974 was the day that President Ford named Shirley the Ambassador to Ghana and it re-called another August 20th to Shirley's mind. It was in 1968 that Shirley, along with four hundred other Americans, were in Czechoslovakia when that Nation fell.

During 1970 Shirley became a U.N. volunteer and visited many countries to make speeches about endangered species and pollution. That year she was also appointed by Secretary of State William Rogers as deputy chairman of the U.S. Delegation to the Conference on Environmental Quality (CEQ). She resigned CEQ in January of 1974, to move on to the job of Ambassador to Ghana.

Some wondered why Shirley allowed herself to travel so much, but when they stopped to realize that her children had grown up normally, with no serious problems and that Charles was proud of his wife's accomplishments, then they could understand and even applaud her. Susan had graduated from Stanford University (art history degree). Charles, Jr. earned an undergraduate degree in political science.

It was in 1972 that Shirley Temple Black found that she had cancer of the breast, and she decided to share her experience with the public and was the first well known woman to do so. Shirley went on radio and television, as well as doing an article for the February 1973 McCall's magazine about the operation and discovery of the cancer.

In 1974 Shirley's name appeared on the Board of Directors for the Del Monte Foods Corporation, the National Wildlife Federation, the United States Association for the United Nations and the National Multiple Sclerosis Society and she was doing work for the Food and Agricultural Organization of the U.N., plus was a member of the U.S. Commission for UNESCO. 1974 was also the year Shirley was named Ambassador to Ghana. Her Ambassadorship was very successful and upon her return to the United States, she was assigned the role of Chief of Protocol for the White House. She would like to return to the United Nations, and we are sure that Shirley Temple Black will continue in her role of helping America and the world wherever she can.

A few items of interest to the Shirley Temple collector: Before Shirley Temple went before the cameras, as a child, one very important item was taken care of . . . to count her curls and be sure there were exactly 56.

In 1972 the Shirley Temple doll collection was donated to the Stanford Children's Hospital and is often on display in the reception area.

Shirley Temple worked on a straight salary, as a child, and has no financial benefit in any of the re-releases of her films.

While she was Ambassordor to Ghana, Shirley was honored by having her face on a coin. She was only the fourth woman to be so honored. The other three were Queen Elizabeth, Indira Ghandi and Martin Luther King's widow, Coretta King.

Recommended as the leading authority on Shirley Temple is Robert Windeler. Two of his books are "Shirley Temple" (1976) and "Shirley Temple Films" (1978).

Revisions

Vol. 1, Page 31 - The **shorter** pitcher is rare, the taller one is most common.
Vol. 1, Page 51 - The 1930's string holder is **plaster**, not plastic.

Doll Marks

COMPOSITION: Some will be marked on both head and body, but many are marked only on the head or the body. An unmarked Ideal Shirley Temple doll is rare.

SHIRLEY TEMPLE

SHIRLEY TEMPLE
IDEAL
N. & T. Co.

Shirley Temple
SHIRLEY TEMPLE

Shirley Temple
IDEAL

VINYL: Marks are on the head and the body.

12"-Ideal Doll-head
ST-12-N

ST-12-N-body

15"-Ideal Doll-head
ST-15-N

ST-15-N-back

17"-Ideal Doll-head
ST-17-1

Ideal Doll-Back
ST-17

19"-Ideal Doll-head
ST-19-1

Ideal Doll-back
ST-19

35"-Ideal Doll-head
ST-35-38-2

Ideal-back
35-5

Copyright 1934
Ideal Doll and Toy
Co.

On dark pink paper label found on INSIDE of "unmarked" Shirley Temple doll by Ideal. Information courtesy The Doll cradle of Merriam, Kansas.

A 20" Shirley Temple, marked both head and body, has been found in the original box and clothes with the following marks: Box: Manufactured by Molly-e's Doll Outfitters, Inc. Hollywood Cinema Fashion Dolls.

Shirley Temple Movies By The Year

This listing is also included in Volume 1, but we wanted to include the other main actors and actresses in these films. because most re-run movies starring Shirley Temple were made by Fox-20th Century Fox, we will begin the listing with 1934.

1934 *Carolina*-Janet Gaynor, Lionel Barrymore, Robert Young.

New Deal Rhythm (For Paramount-musical featurette)-Buddy Rogers, Marjorie Main.

Change of Heart-Janet Gaynor, Charles Farrell, James Dunn, Ginger Rogers.

Little Miss Marker (Paramount)-Adolphe Menjou, Dorothy Dell, Charles Bickford.

Stand Up and Cheer-Warner Baxter, Madge Evans.

Baby Take A Bow-James Dunn, Claire Trevor.

Now and Forever (Paramount)-Gary Cooper, Carole Lombard.

Bright Eyes-James Dunn, Jane Darwell with a small partner Jane Withers.

The Little Colonel-Lionel Barrymore, Evelyn Venable.

1935 *Our Little Girl*-Rosemary Ames, Joel McCray.

Curly Top-John Boles, Rochelle Hudson.

The Littlest Rebel-John Boles, Jack Holt, Karen Morley.

1936 *Captain January*-Guy Kibbee, June Lang, Slim Summerfield, Buddy Ebsen.

The Poor Little Rich Girl-Alice Faye, Gloria Stuart, Jack Haley.

Dimples-Frank Morgan, Helen Westley.

Stowaway-Robert Young, Alice Faye.

1937 *Wee Willie Winkie*-Victor McLaglen, C. Aubrey Smith, June Lang.

Heidi-Jean Hersholt, Arthur Treacher, Helen Westley.

1938 *Rebecca of Sunnybrook Farm*-Randolph Scott, Jack Haley, Gloria Stuart.

Just Around The Corner-Charles Farrell, Joan Davis.

Little Miss Broadway-George Murphy, Jimmy Durante, Phyllis Brooks.

1939 *The Little Princess*-Richard Greene, Anita Louise.

Susannah of the Mounties-Randolph Scott, Margaret Lockwood.

Composition. All original for *Stand Up and Cheer*. This is one of the earliest dolls. Note looser hairdo. She is 15" tall and marked only with Ideal on head. This doll is referred to in "Shirley's Dolls and Related Delights" (Prototype) by Loraine Burdick, pages 13 and 14. A very rare doll. 1934. Courtesy Meisinger Collection.

27" Composition. All original and has original box. Green pleated organdy from *Baby Take A Bow*. 1934. Rayon tag (peach background). Courtesy Meisinger Collection.

17" All original composition, except shoes. Rayon label. From *Stand Up and Cheer*. 1934. Designed by Mollye Goldman and came in various colors, such as red, green and blue. Courtesy Meisinger Collection.

16" Fully marked composition in original tagged Shirley Temple trenchcoat. Ca. 1934-35. Courtesy Rita Dubas. Photo by John DeLuca.

13" Composition in blue organdy *Baby Take A Bow*. Rayon tag. 1934. Courtesy Meisinger Collection.

25" Composition. All original with heavier cotton dress (plaid) from *Bright Eyes*. 1934. Courtesy Meisinger Collection.

13" Doll in trunk. Composition. Two extra outfits, shoes and jewelry. Original pin. All tagged. 1935. Courtesy Rita Dubas. Photo by John DeLuca.

16" Composition *Heidi*. All original. Shown in ads of 1930's as Heidi, but is shown in 1936 catalog before Heidi was made and actually looks like dress from *The Littlest Rebel*. 1935-1936.

13" *Curly Top*. All composition, original and in original box. This dress came in other shades but this aqua with brown is one of the nicest. 1935. Courtesy Meisinger Collection.

16" Composition. All original with original box. Aqua with brown organdy. From *Curly Top*. Rayon tag. 1935. Courtesy Meisinger Collection.

22" Composition that is all original in original box. White organdy with red dots which are different. Half solid red and half dotted. Woven cotton NRA tag. From *Curly Top*. 1935. Courtesy Meisinger Collection.

Back view 22" to show curls. Courtesy Meisinger Collection.

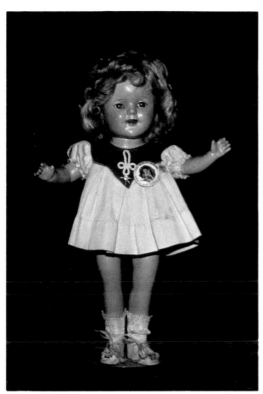

16" Composition in yellow cotton pique. *Our Littel Girl*. Rayon tag. 1935, Courtesy Meisinger Collection.

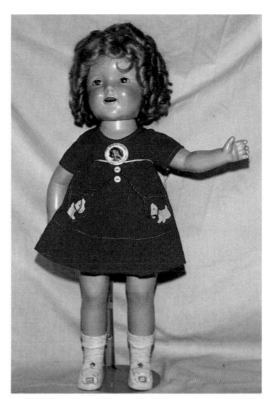

20" Composition. All original red cotton dress from *Our Little Girl*. Rayon tag. 1935. Courtesy Meisinger Collection.

20" This doll was mint in the box and included with her was this RUBBER raincape with collar and tam. 1935. Courtesy Alma Carmichael.

27" All original and mint composition Shirley dressed from the movie *Little Colonel*. 1935. Courtesy Rita Dubas. Photo by John DeLuca.

20" *Poor Little Rich Girl.* Composition and fully marked. Came in original box. Original pin. Red velveteen coat trimmed in red/white dotted cotton, with hat. Wears burgundy red sailor dress under coat from same movie. All clothes are tagged. 1936. Courtesy Rita Dubas. Photo by John DeLuca.

20" Composition. All original with original box. Red Cotton pique from *Poor Little Rich Girl.* Rayon tag. 1936. Courtesy Carol Meisinger.

17" Ranger Doll (Cowgirl). Mint and all original, including her hat and gun. 1936. Courtesy Alma Carmichael.

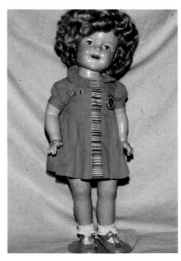

16" Composition in blue cotton sailor dress from *Poor Little Rich Girl.* 1936. Courtesy Meisinger Collection.

22" Composition. All original green cotton dress from *Stowaway.* 1936. Courtesy Meisinger Collection.

18" *Wee Willie Winkie*. All composition, fully marked, tagged and pinned. 1937. Courtesy Rita Dubas. Photo by John Deluca.

20" Bluebird. Composition. Fully marked. Came in the original "Stern Bros." box. Polished cotton and organdy, with white net overlay on yoke. Felt bluebird. Original button. Could have been a salesman sample. 1940. Courtesy Rita Dubas. Photo by John DeLuca.

20" Shirley baby with molded hair. All original. Sweater made from old pattern. Courtesy Rita Dubas. Photo by John DeLuca.

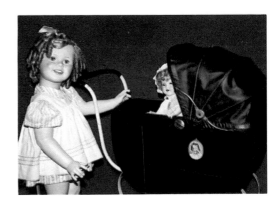

35" Vinyl Shirley Temple wearing original "Patti Playpal" outfit. The carriage (32" high/wide overall) has a painted wood body, stencil line design, picture of Shirley in oval, name on hub caps and hood knob, also marked: Genuine/Shirley Temple/20th Century Fox Film Star/Whitney-Ideal/Doll Carriage, decal on diaper compartment door. In carriage is 16" all original Shirley Baby with flirty eyes. Courtesy Fay & Jimmy Rodolfos.

27" Wigged Shirley Temple baby. Flirty eyes. Sweater made form old pattern. Courtesy Rita Dubas. Photo by John DeLuca.

15" Tall statue of chalk. "Movie Baby" inscribed on the front of the base. Courtesy Loretta Zablotny.

Shows two 12" vinyl dolls of 1958-59 with original out-fits. Replaced shoes. Courtesy Meisinger Collection.

12" Original 1958-59 vinyl Shirley dolls. Shoes have been replaced. Courtesy Meisinger Collection.

12" All original doll except shoes have been replaced on doll on the right. 1958. Courtesy Meisinger Collection.

1958-59 Vinyl Shirley's that are original. Shoes have been replaced on doll on the right. Courtesy Meisinger Collection.

12" Vinyl 1958-59 Shirley in original ballerina outfit. Courtesy Meisinger Collection.

12" Vinyl Shirleys in original dresses. The shoes have been replaced. Courtesy Meisinger Collection.

15" Vinyl in blue and white cotton dress, which may be for a Toni doll. Courtesy Meisinger Collection.

17" Vinyl in original outfits. The same dresses were in several different colors. Courtesy Meisinger Collection.

17" Vinyl with pink nylon. All original. 1957. Courtesy Meisinger Collection.

Two slightly different pins from the 1950's Shirley Temple dolls. Courtesy Meisinger Collection.

15" Vinyl. Another variation of Heidi, as there were several. All original cotton dress. Courtesy Meisinger Collection.

15" Vinyl Little Red Riding Hood. All original blue cotton dress, white nylon apron and red gabardine hood. Courtesy Meisinger Collection.

12" Vinyl Shirleys. Not sure if the left outfit is original or not. The shoes have been replaced. Courtesy Meisinger Collection.

12" Vinyl Shirleys in original outfits. Shoes have been replaced on the doll on the left. Courtesy Meisinger Collection.

12" Shirleys that are vinyl and from 1958-59. Both have original dresses, but have replaced shoes. Courtesy Meisinger Collection.

12" Vinyl. Left is original except shoes. The right pinafore is replaced on an original outfit. Courtesy Meisinger Collection.

12" In original outfits. The shoes have been replaced. Courtesy Meisinger Collection.

Shows two 15" vinyl Shirley's. It is not known if the outfits are original or not. Courtesy Meisinger Collection.

15" Cinderella. Vinyl. All original. 1961. White dress of lace and nylon with red flocked cotton top. Courtesy Meisinger Collection.

35" Vinyl with jointed wrists. Dress not original but Shirley Temple Style. Courtesy Meisinger Collection.

Shows six of the 35" vinyl/plastic Shirley Temples. All are original and all are in the collection of Thelma Kimble.

15" Vinyl. All original blue dress with white cotton collar, sleeves and pantalets, red apron. Little Bo Peep. Courtesy Marge Meisinger.

16" Wax Shirley Temple made by Bobi Langhau of Oshkosh, WI. Dated and signed on back of head. Dolls made in Limited Editions. Dressed by Bobi.

1973 Shirley Temple and box, plus back of box. Courtesy Meisinger Collection.

9" Bisque head with composition body. Molded/-painted hair, shoes and sox. Doll and outfit marked: Japan. Outfit is trimmed in shells, shell basket. Doll glued to silver base much like Kewpies were. Only arms can move. Made for Atlantic City, N.J. store display. About 1936. Courtesy Rita Dubas. Photo by John DeLuca.

4" Bisque reproduction. Courtesy Meisinger Collection.

32" *Littlest Rebel* made by Mildred Burkeman of Encinitas, CA. Ball jointed body with bisque head. Courtesy Millie Busch.

22" Sculptured cloth doll made by Shirley Ann Brannigan of California. Courtesy Millie Busch.

13" Wax portrait of 1973 by doll artist Carol Carlton. Dressed as Little Colonel in organdy. Painted features. A beautiful likeness. Courtesy Rita Dubas. Photo by John DeLuca.

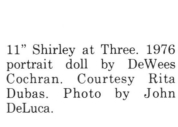

11" Shirley at Three. 1976 portrait doll by DeWees Cochran. Courtesy Rita Dubas. Photo by John DeLuca.

Shirley Temple made by doll artist for the Enchanted Doll House (Mass.). Porcelain bisque head and limbs, cloth body. Courtesy Millie Busch.

20" "Rebecca of Sunnybrook Farm" made by Mildred Burkeman of Encinitas, CA. Bisque head. Courtesy Millie Busch.

10" Shirley Temple look-a-like and marked "Little Natalie". She was made by the Sun Rubber Company. One piece rubber body and limbs. Was a child's squeeze toy. Courtesy Loretta Zablotny.

18" Shirley Temple. "Oilcloth"-type torso and arms. Flesh tone cloth legs with sewn on white stockings and pale blue velvet shoes attached. Molded and pressed face with brown oil painted eyes and inset lashes. Mohair wig. Original. Doll and clothes made by Mollye. Courtesy Meisinger Collection.

Cloth Shirley Temple. All hand made by Jean Miller, New Hope, AL. Courtesy Phyllis Houston.

31

27" Composition by Ideal, but not a Shirley Temple. Wears outfit she came in. Original Shirley dress and underwear from *Curly Top*. Courtesy Meisinger Collection.

35" Vinyl that is not a Shirley Temple. Lighter weight plastic, came in authentic Shirley clothes. Doll unmarked. Courtesy Meisinger Collection.

13" Composition by Ideal. Red hair, not a Shirley Temple, but wears original dress and underwear with part of Shirley Temple rayon tag. Courtesy Meisinger Collection.

20" Ideal marked doll that is not a Shirley Temple. Ideal also made several different babies that looked very much like a Shirley Baby, but were not. Courtesy Meisinger Collection.

18" Composition Alexander's *Little Colonel*. All original cotton dimity. Tag: *Little Colonel* Alexander Doll Co. Although not a Shirley Temple, she is important enough to show. Courtesy Meisinger Collection.

22" Japanese composition Shirley Temple. Replaced dress. Courtesy Millie Busch.

Boxed Doll clothes. 1936. For 20" doll, included dress, hanger, slip, extra doll button & photo. Photo has ad for baby Shirley on back. Courtesy Rita Dubas. Photo by John DeLuca.

20" Composition dressed in plaid rain-coat with matching hat and umbrella. Designed by Mollye and on market April, 1935. Courtesy Meisinger Collection.

15" In crochet outfit made form the American Thread Co. #85 pattern. (Shown in black and white section.) Designs for child's dress and doll dress by Bertha Natino. Courtesy Meisinger Collection.

16" Composition red & white dimity dress and hat. No information, but designed by Mollye. Courtesy Meisinger Collection.

16" Composition in yellow dotted lawn dress. Braid trim. Also came in blue. Courtesy Meisinger Collection.

Ballerina outfit and sailor suit for 12"
1958 vinyl Shirley doll. Courtesy
Meisinger Collection.

Two boxed outfits for the 12" vinyl
doll. Courtesy Meisinger Collection.

Two dresses, one for the 17" and the
other for 12" vinyl doll. Courtesy
Meisinger Collection.

Extra outfits for the vinyl Shirley's.
Not sure the left dress is for Shirley,
but it is an Ideal dress. Courtesy Meisinger Collection.

1973 Clothes boxes.

A jacket worn by Shirley in a movie. Cloth tag says "Shirley Temple". Paper bag pinned to it says "22-S Temple. Cloth tag says "A.V.-S. Temple/1X-Xs. Courtesy Millie Busch.

Celanese rayon taffeta Shirley Temple dress. Size 1. Marked "Nanette Toddler Dress-Shirley Temple Brand" and also "Shirley Temple, 20th Century Film Star". Courtesy Millie Busch.

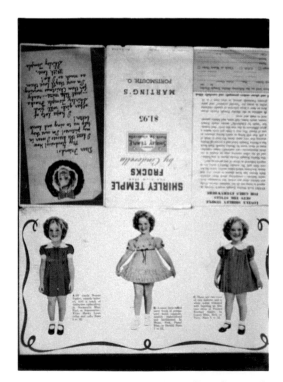

Brochure showing the dresses called "Shirley Temple Frocks" and made by Cinderella. 1930's. Courtesy Thelma Kimble.

Both are taffeta dresses of the 1930's. Both were made by Nanette. Courtesy Meisinger Collection.

Child's dress size 3. 1930's. Organdy. Courtesy Rita Dubas. Photo by John DeLuca.

Size 2 Nanette Shirley Temple dress. Courtesy Meisinger Collection.

Cotton Shirley Temple dress. Size 3. 1930's Marked "Cinderella" and "Shirley Temple". Courtesy Millie Busch.

Plastic and metal barrette. 1930's. Courtesy Rita Dubas. Photo by John DeLuca.

Handerkerchiefs, boxed. 3 different. 1930's Courtesy Rita Dubas. Photo by John DeLuca.

Red purse and mirror by Pyramid. Has original label. Courtesy Meisinger Collection.

This is an old charm bracelet with Scotty dog, heart with incised name of Shirley Temple and replica of Shirley in a dancing dress. Courtesy Meisinger Collection.

Child's charm bracelet. 1930's. See black and white section for different charms that were available. Courtesy Rita Dubas. Photo by John DeLuca.

Old Sterling cloisonné bracelet from Denmark. Excellent quality head of Shirley with dark blue trim. Courtesy Meisinger Collection.

Top of box that holds the Shirley head necklace. No makers name is on the box, only the number 7209G. Courtesy Meisinger Collection.

Child's bracelet that is old and of excellent quality. Matches necklace in box. Courtesy Meisinger Collection.

This necklace matches the bracelet, but was sold separately. Photo of box top above this picture. Courtesy Meisinger Collection.

2" Shirley Temple pin of heavy plastic type celluloid. Hand painted, in oil, flowers and shows the pin the tiny door closed. 1930's. Courtesy Laura Cleghorn. Photo by Dretske's of Waukegan.

Shows the pin with the tiny door open to reveal a photo of Shirley Temple.

1¼" Brooch from Holland. Heavy celluloid, but has all the appearance of plastic. Small cut window with paper pasted on back with photo of Shirley Temple. In tiny heart shaped box and it is not known if box is original to pin. Courtesy Meisinger Collection.

This is one of the pins that could be ordered from 20th Century Fox. (See black & white section for all the charms.) There was a bear on one end of this pin that is missing. Courtesy Alma Carmichael.

Shows three various pinback pins that are currently on the market and available through antique publications.

They are made to look old, even to the rust on the backs. Some are advertised as old "store stock" and this is very questionable. Courtesy Meisinger Collection.

Advertised as "old store stock", this pin is interesting in that it says, "New Theatre WFBR/Shirley Temple Club". The age of the pin, and the origin is unknown. Courtesy Meisinger Collection.

Pinback type pin available to Shirley Temple Fans. Courtesy Meisinger Collection.

Ali Baba & The Forty Thieves was sponsored by Breck Shampoo on the "Shirley Temple Storybook" (NBC) Wednesday, November 12, 1958 and this is a medal from Breck. Courtesy Meisinger Collection.

Shows the reverse side of the Breck medal. Courtesy Meisinger Collection.

This is a beautiful life-like painting done by Connie Marshall. She works in charcoal and her paintings are in various sizes. This one is a large 18" by 24". (Author).

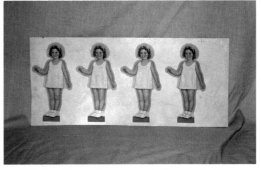

Paper doll proofs from printers. 1935 for Saalfield. Courtesy Meisinger Collection.

Shirley Temple paper doll proofs from printers stock. No. 1761 for Saalfield. 1937. Courtesy Meisinger Collection.

Christmas Book paper doll. Courtesy Meisinger Collection.

Christmas Book #1770 by Saalfield in 1937. Courtesy Meisinger Collection.

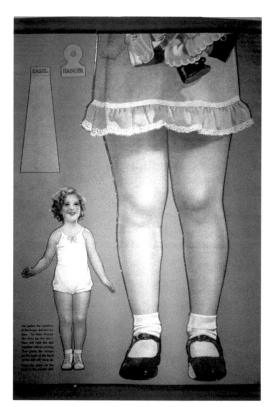

34" Paper doll that is mint and uncut. Top half is the front and bottom half is on the back cover. 1936. Saalfield. Courtesy Meisinger Collection.

Back cover of the 34" paper doll by Saalfield, showing the 9½" that goes with this set. Courtesy Meisinger Collection.

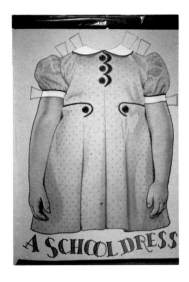

This shows the six inside pages that go with the 34" paper doll. Courtesy Meisinger Collection.

1939 Saalfield paper doll book #1782 with two dolls, one on the front cover and one on the back cover. Courtesy Meisinger Collection.

Back cover doll for the Saalfield set #1782. Courtesy Meisinger Collection.

This page shows the entire inside of the Saalfield paper dolls of 1939 (#1782). Courtesy Meisinger Collection.

This entire page shows the full contents of the 1934 (MCMXX-XIV) #280 paper dolls and the clothes by Saalfield. Courtesy Alma Carmichael.

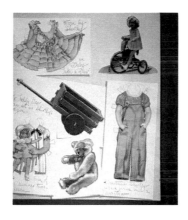

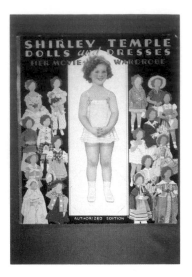

This is the Sallfield boxed paper doll set of 1935 (MCMXXXV) #1719. Shows the box top, also. Courtesy Alma Carmichael.

Paper doll in the Shirley Temple Annual from Great Britain. The book is shown in Volume 1 on page 54 and is the second (middle) book on top of the page. Courtesy Meisinger Collection.

This is the Dell paper doll Birthday Book (shown in Volume 1, page 43). 1935. The book contains games, puzzles and over 40 photos of Shirley in addition to the paper doll. Courtesy Meisinger Collection.

An additional page of paper doll clothes from the Dell Birthday book. Courtesy Meisinger Collection.

This page of paper doll clothes is from the 1935 Dell Birthday Book. Courtesy Meisinger Collection.

This is the paper doll from the Saalfield set #303 of 1937 and shows some of the clothes. Courtesy Alma Carmichael.

Additional clothes from the Saalfield #303 set. Courtesy Alma Carmichael.

These items are from some of the 1930's paper doll sets. Courtesy Alma Carmichael.

Set #1715 by Saalfield. 1935. This shows some of the clothes from the set and one of the dolls. Courtesy Alma Carmichael.

Shows doll made by Saalfield (1935) with clothes that have both fronts and backs. Number of book unknown. Courtesy Alma Carmichael.

Paper dolls from Spain and marked: Ediciones, Barcelona. These are No. 1 and 9. The paper used is the poor quality "pulp" kind. Courtesy Meisinger Collection.

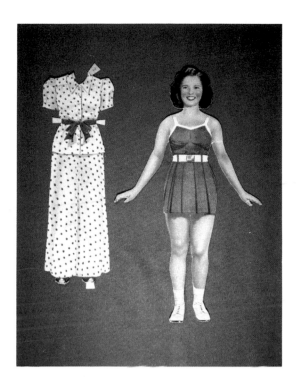

This page contains the Saalfield paper doll book of 1942. #2425. There were two 10½" paper dolls in this set. Courtesy Alma Carmichael.

Paper dolls from Spain and marked: Ediciones, Barcelona. These are No. 1 and 9. The paper used is the poor quality "pulp" kind. Courtesy Meisinger Collection.

Spanish paper dolls. Year and maker are unknown. Courtesy Meisinger Collection.

Framed cut out of Shirley Temple that had been dressed including ribbon bands on the socks. Also has cut out of Shirley watering flowers. Courtesy Meisinger Collection.

A cut and framed Shirley Temple paper doll. Gown is from *Little Colonel*. Courtesy Millie Busch.

Current paper doll that is boxed with both the figure and the box marked: 1976 Shirley Temple Black. Made by Whitman. Courtesy Meisinger Collection.

The Whitman paper doll book #1986 that is currently on the market. Both book and figure are marked: 1976 Shirley Temple Black. Courtesy Meisinger Collection.

Quaker Puffed Wheat comic page ad. Boston Sun Globe of March 6, 1938. It is large half page newspaper size. Courtesy Rita Dubas. Photo by John DeLuca.

Early 1930's Gimbels Dept. Store catalog and order blank. Courtesy Meisinger Collection.

Quaker Puffed Wheat comic page of the Boston Sun Globe of April 25, 1937. Large half page newspaper size. Courtesy Rita Dubas. Photo by John DeLuca.

Back cover of the National Geographic Magazine of December 1936 to show how other companies used the Shirley Temple influence. Courtesy Meisinger Collection.

Art Photo #66 (Great Britain) with greetings for sixth Birthday. Shown with original "picture window" envelope. Courtesy Meisinger Collection.

Art Photo Postcard (Great Britain) #36-1. Also #8584C and is a Birthday Greeting Card. Courtesy Meisinger Collection.

Book "Littlest Rebel" 1935. Shows the dust jacket, which is generally not found with the book. Courtesy Rita Dubas. Photo by John DeLuca.

Dutch booklet of "Kapitein Januari" by Rein Valkhoff. Tells the story of *Captain January* and contains many photos from the movie. Courtesy Meisinger Collection.

The Films of Shirley Temple by Robert Windeler. 1978. Courtesy Alma Carmichael.

Coloring Set #1718. 1935. Saalfield. Loose pages, boxed with crayons. Original price was $.10. Courtesy Rita Dubas. Photo by John DeLuca.

Drawing Book #1725. Hardcover.
1935. From Saalfield Library.
Original price tag is $.25. Courtesy
Rita Dubas. Photo by John DeLuca.

Coloring Box #1731. 1935. From
Saalfield Library. Courtesy Rita
Dubas. Photo by John DeLuca.

Pastime Box #1732. 1937. Saalfield.
Four books: #1732-A: Favorite
Games, #1732-B: Favorite Sewing
Cards, #1732-C: Favorite Puzzles,
#1732-D: Favorite Coloring Book.
Courtesy Rita Dubas. Photo by John
DeLuca.

Coloring Book #1735. Hardcover.
1935. From Saalfield Library.
Original price was $.50. Courtesy Rita
Dubas. Photo by John DeLuca.

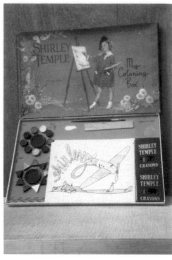

This Shirley Temple "My Coloring Box" is #1740 and made by Saalfield. Courtesy Loretta Zablotny.

Shirley Temple Drawing Set with coloring book, #1738 by Saalfield in 1935. Courtesy Meisinger Collection.

Coloring book with red cover. By Saalfield in 1936. Courtesy Meisinger Collection.

Western Publishing Composition Books. 1930's. Courtesy Rita Dubas. Photo by John DeLuca.

Screenland Movie Magazine cover of April 1936. Courtesy Alma Carmichael.

Modern Screen Magazine cover of July 1935. Courtesy Alma Carmichael.

Cover for the Sunday Mirror Magazine Section (New York) and dated December 20, 1936. Courtesy Meisinger Collection.

The English publication "Picture Show" of December 11, 1937. The cover is titled "Shirley Temple catches Father Christmas Napping". Courtesy Meisinger Collection.

Picture Show magazine from England has Shirley on the cover and a large coverage of *Poor Little Rich Girl*, plus a giveaway photo in center. December 26, 1936 issue. Courtesy Meisinger Collection.

Page 299 from the Sketch Magazine of February 15, 1939. Along with the photo is the caption describing her in *Just Around The Corner* when she played the part of Penny Hale. Courtesy Meisinger Collection.

"A Rienda Suelta" is a Spanish pulp magazine put out by Ediciones Biblioteca Films in Barcelona and Madrid. 1940's. Has a center section of photos. Courtesy Meisinger Collection.

This special issue of Modern Screen contains many photos of Shirley Temple. April 1949. Courtesy Meisinger Collection.

THE POOR LITTLE RICH GIRL.

SHIRLEY TEMPLE'S latest is the Twentieth-Century Fox film "The Poor Little Rich Girl," at the New Gallery. The fascinating baby is as gay and charming as ever she was in "Captain January"—in which film this portrait shows her.

PAINTING BY CHARLES BINGER.

This page from Sketch Magazine shows a drawing by Charles Binger of Shirley as she was in *Captain January* and is a description of *The Poor Little Rich Girl*. Dated September 16, 1936. Courtesy Meisinger Collection.

Philadelphia Inquirer "Picture Parade" covers. Left: Easter April 18, 1938 and right: December 25, 1938. Courtesy Rita Dubas. Photo by John DeLuca.

New York Sunday News Cover. Left: June 12, 1938 and right is December 7, 1941, on Pearl Harbor Day. Courtesy Rita Dubas. Photo by John DeLuca.

Cover of the December 13, 1936 Milwaukee Journal. Courtesy Meisinger Collection.

This is a lobby still advertising the movie *The Blue Bird* and copyrighted in 1939. Courtesy Meisinger Collection.

Lobby posters. 14" x 17". Clockwise-left to right: *Our Little Girl*-1935, *Little Colonel*-1935, *Our Little Girl*. Courtesy Rita Dubas. Photo by John DeLuca.

Our Little Girl lobby poster. Copyright is 1935. Courtesy Meisinger Collection.

Original oil painting movie poster of Heidi. 1937. 28" x 40". Courtesy Rita Dubas. Photo by John DeLuca.

30" x 40" Christmas Poster. Marked: 1935 Twentieth Century Fox Film Corp. Country of origin, U.S.A. Hand colored. Courtesy Rita Dubas. Photo by John DeLuca.

30" x 40" Christmas Poster. Marked: 1934, Fox Film Corp. Country of origin, U.S.A. "Merry Christmas and a Happy New Year from the management" Courtesy Rita Dubas. Photo by John DeLuca.

Shirley Temple Limited Edition poster. 1977 and personally signed "Shirley Temple". Courtesy Meisinger Collection.

Press Review booklet of the movie *The Little Princess* at the Carthay Circle Theatre on February 17, 1939. Insides show the full cast and production staff and information on the film and the use of Technicolor. Courtesy Meisinger Collection.

1950's scrapbook showing Shirley's family. Courtesy Meisinger Collection.

Ad from the Espinel Theatre for Miss Annie Rooney (1942) and advertised as "I Want To Be A Women". Also carries ad for "Dual" new phonographic equipment (of recent importation) indispensible in every home as a compliment to your radio". Translation courtesy Chris Paez.

1974 Ideal Toy Catalogue showing the Shirley Temple doll of that year. Courtesy Meisinger Collection.

Shows a page from the 1974 Ideal Toy Catalog with the Movie outfits for the Shirley Temple doll. Courtesy Meisinger Collection.

8 x 10 hand-tinted and autographed photo received by a fan in the 1930's. Courtesy Meisinger Collection.

Autographed picture, in Heidi costume and color, made in 1937 and signed: "To Margaret, Love Shirley Temple 1937". Courtesy Millie Busch.

Photo given away with the Film Pictorial on July 31st, 1937. Courtesy Meisinger Collection.

Personally signed photo by Shirley Temple Black to the Meisingers. (1977). Courtesy Meisinger Collection.

TV GUIDE Cover Portrait

Cover of the 1959 TV Guide. Whoever owned the copyrights of this cover made up 10 or 11 of these "Shirley Temple Portraits". 11 x 14 with overall size 16 x 20.

Dresser scarf from the 1930's. Iron on patterns were available, as well as the pre-printed items. Courtesy Meisinger Collection.

This is a tablecloth that was pre-printed. Dates from the 1930's. Courtesy Meisinger Collection.

This embroidering looks as if it were meant to be a framed picture. The figure itself, looks as if done by a child, where the rest was completed by an adult. Dates from the 1930's. Courtesy Meisinger Collection.

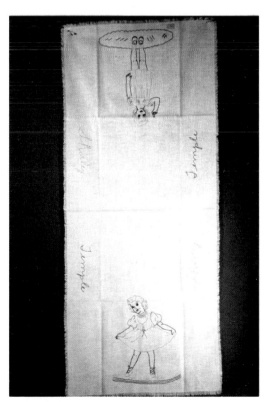

This 1930's dresser scarf has the name Shirley Temple embroidered on the sides. The thread used was very thin and pale. Courtesy Meisinger Collection.

A dresser scarf/and or towel that ia all hand done and dates from the 1930's. Courtesy Meisinger Collection.

"Work With Yarn" #1750. 1936. Saalfield. Yarn, scissors, sewing kit, crayons, 12 pictures. Original price was $1.00. Courtesy Rita Dubas. Photo by John DeLuca.

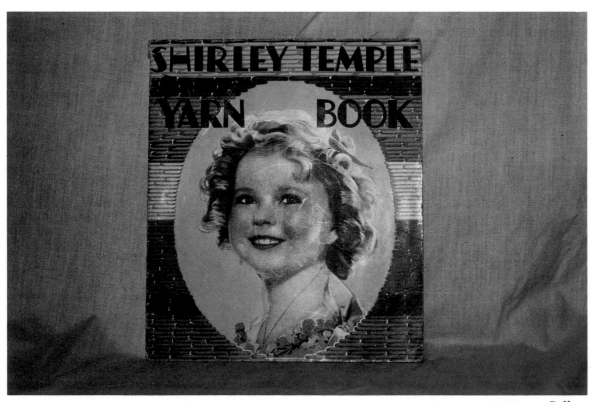

Yarn book #1777. 1936 by Saalfield. Companion to "Work With Yarn". Courtesy Meisinger Collection.

1930's balloon made of rubber and 10" tall. Look-a-like face of Shirley Temple, wearing coon-skin cap and an outfit drawn on the balloon to resemble the fringed outfit she wore in *Susannah of the Mounties* (1939). Courtesy Loretta Zoblotny.

This item is also shown in the Black & White section. Game made in Japan of the type where you try to get the marbles into the eyes. The head drawing is similar to the mask that was also made in Japan. Courtesy Rita Dubas. Photo by John DeLuca.

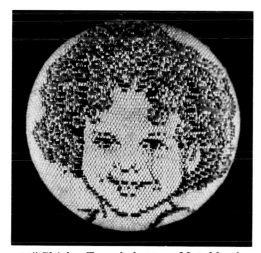

½" Shirley Temple button. Metal back with loop for sewing to material. Cloth center, finely embroidered with silk thread through material. (Machine made). 1930's. Courtesy Meisinger Collection.

Little Colonel Game by Selchow & Righter Co. 1935. Not authentic Shirley Temple, but marketed at time of release of the movie. Courtesy Meisinger Collection.

Shows the inside of "Little Colonel" Game. Courtesy Meisinger Collection.

A set of child's pen and pencil set. Both have Shirley Temple incised on holder (clip) and also imprinted deeply into the side of barrels. Courtesy Meisinger Collection.

This was one of the center pieces made by Arline and Mel Roth for the Shirley Temple Luncheon at the National Convention of the United Federation of Doll Clubs in Denver, August 1978. The Luncheon Theme was "Good Ship Lollipop." Courtesy Meisinger Collection.

Pink plastic tea set of 1959 is unusual because the plates and saucers have a flower design and not the usual Shirley Temple monogram. Courtesy Loretta Zablotny.

Shows 30 ft. of the April 1, 1935 display of Mollye's Hollywood Film Fashions on display at the Gimbel's Store of New York City. Many of the early Shirley Temple items are on display and recognizable. Courtesy Meisinger Collection.

Photo of Shirley Temple Black, along with Marge and Earl Meisinger, taken in Chicago. 1977. Courtesy Meisinger Collection.

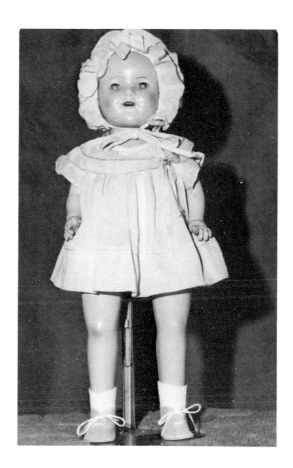

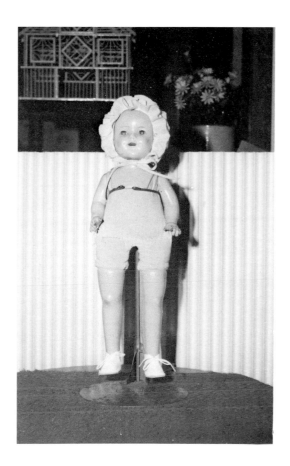

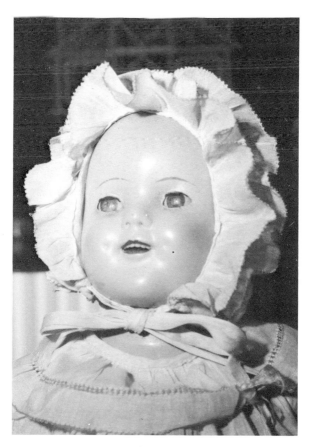

19" Shirley Temple. Has spray painted yellow hair. Never wigged. Cloth body with composition legs, arms and head. Sleep eyes, dimples and open mouth with six teeth. Original clothes. Composition shoulderplate. Ca. 1939. Courtesy Ruth Lane.

This is the sample of *Little Colonel* dress 1934-1935 made by Mollye. Ideal ordered from this sample. Courtesy Meisinger Collection.

20" All lithographed cloth with pink skin tones and good detail. The fingers are curled under (printed). The yellow yarn hair has uniquely formed curls. It is not known if this is meant to be a Shirley Temple doll or not, but has the appearance of Shirley. Date is unknown. Courtesy Meisinger Collection.

20" Shirley Temple baby shown in the smallest carriage made. The carriage is made of wicker, has the name of Shirley Temple on the hubs and photo on the sides. Courtesy Rita Dubas.

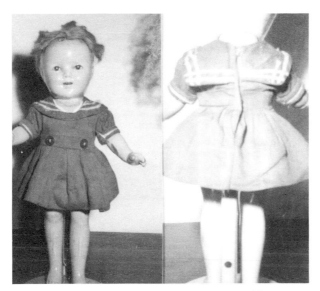

This 13" Shirley doll is wearing a blue cotton pique dress with white sailor trim and two red buttons. The doll is marked both on the head and the body. The wig is almost worn off. Designed and made by Mollye. Dress was on market April 1935. Courtesy Eloise Godfrey.

36" Shirley Temples. Both original, but one on the right has a slightly different look and her body is of light weight plastic. She has jointed wrists. She also measures ½" less around the cheeks. Marks: Ideal Doll/ST-35-38-2, on head and Ideal, in oval/35 on back. Both dolls courtesy Marge Meisinger.

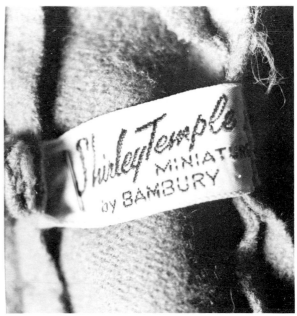

Miniature coat that is well made and fits a 12" doll. Light brown wool, velvet collar. Tag reads: Shirley Temple miniature by Bambury. Courtesy Meisinger Collection.

This is a close up of the tag found in coat. Courtesy Meisinger Collection.

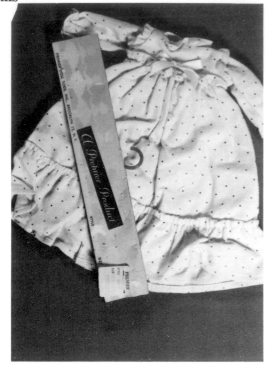

Nightgown made by Premier Products and sold for "Shirley 12", style #3079. 1957-1958. Came in pink and blue. Courtesy Meisinger Collection.

18" Composition. White fur coat with pink lining. Courtesy Meisinger Collection.

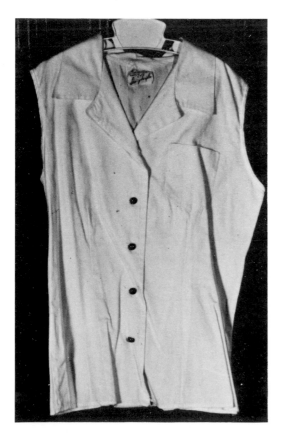

Blouse is size 10 and a Shirley Temple design by "Cinderella". Courtesy Meisinger Collection.

Hairbow. "Shirley Temple Midget Bows with Bobby Pins". Had two silk bows. 1930's. Courtesy Rita Dubas. Photo by John DeLuca.

Child's purse by Pyramid. Enameled Ship's Wheel. Tagged. 1930's. Courtesy Rita Dubas. Photo by John DeLuca.

1958 Shirley Temple's child purse. Measures 2 7/8" by 4". Courtesy Maxine Heitt.

Hankie designed and made by LaVaughn Johnston. Courtesy Meisinger Collection.

Hankerchiefs in box. Also shown in color section. Courtesy Maxine Heitt.

Underwear tag. 1930's. Courtesy Rita Dubas. Photo by John DeLuca.

Other side of the Underwear Tag. 1930's.

5" Tall salt figure in riding habit. Has Shirley curls. Ca. 1930's. Courtesy Meisinger Collection.

Two old salt bisque figures and center is a new figure from Mexico of unknown material. Courtesy Meisinger Collection.

Veterans of Foreign War bust. Plaster and is child size. Wears cap and cape of the Jr. V.F.W. Shirley posed in this outfit in 1934. Signed and dated: "J. Erker. 1937". Intaglio eyes. Other markes obliterated. No other information. Courtesy Rita Dubas. Photo by John DeLuca.

3 Salt bisque figures. No marks.
Courtesy Meisinger Collection.

Bronzed plaque, probably of the
1930's. Says Shirley Temple around
the edge. Curls and face are carved in
stand out from the plaque. Bronzed
baby shoe did not come with it.
Courtesy Millie Busch.

Pin made by and available from Kay
Bransky. Courtesy Meisinger Collection.

Another pose used on new pins by Kay
Bransky. Courtesy Meisinger Collection.

This page and part of the next show a few of the charms that were available in the 1930's. The only marks are: S.T. Jewelry, Inc. Shown in color in catalog. Courtesy Meisinger Collection.

Charm
No. 284

TOY AUTOMOBILE

In her auto, up and down,
Shirley drives in Movie-town,
While the children clap and say
"Here comes Shirley, Hip,
Hooray."

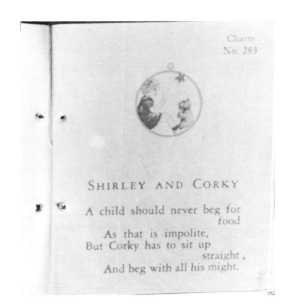

Charm
No. 283

SHIRLEY AND CORKY

A child should never beg for
food
As that is impolite,
But Corky has to sit up
straight.
And beg with all his might.

Charm
No. 268

DOLL HOUSE

"In my pretty doll house"
Shirley says, "You'll see
Lots of little dollies
Just like me."

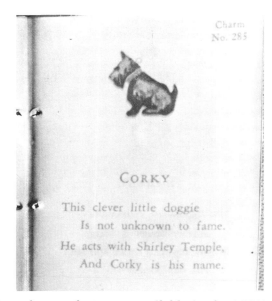

Charm
No. 285

CORKY

This clever little doggie
Is not unknown to fame.
He acts with Shirley Temple,
And Corky is his name.

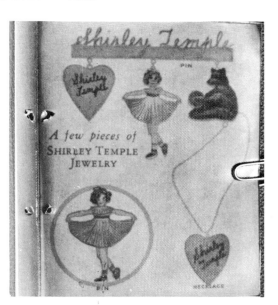

More charms that were available in the 1930's. The last photo shows the charms/pins and necklace that
was also available. Courtesy Meisinger Collection.

New and current necklace. One thing that is good about these necklaces is that they look very new and are not as apt to be passed off as older ones. Courtesy Meisinger Collection.

New ring that matches necklaces. The rings are adjustable. Courtesy Meisinger Collection.

Another new necklace. Each have matching rings. Courtesy Meisinger Collection.

This is a new ring that is currently being sold and matches a necklace. Courtesy Meisinger Collection.

This is an old mirror with a different picture on it. Courtesy Alma Carmichael.

This watch is new and available through Antique publications. It is a pocket watch with photo of Shirley in *Little Colonel*. There are no marks on the watch. Courtesy Meisinger Collection.

1¼" Celluloid charm of the 1930's. The dress is blue-greenish and the shoes are red. No marks. Courtesy Meisinger Collection.

The charm with the cut out head of Shirley Temple was shown in gold in Volume 1. This one is silver. Courtesy Alma Carmichael. This item is now being reproduced, caution is advised **if** purchasing as "old".

Sterling Silver charm from the Movieland Wax Museum. Courtesy Meisinger Collection.

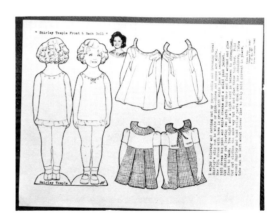

This page shows some of the Shirley Temple paper dolls designed and drawn by Emma Terry. Currently available. Courtesy Meisinger Collection.

Paper doll by Emma Terry, which also includes a calendar for 1976 and 1977. Courtesy Meisinger Collection.

1976 Bicentennial paper doll and Christmas Greeting card made and sent by Emma Terry. Courtesy Meisinger Collection.

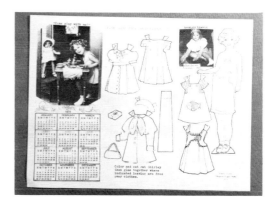

Paper dolls by Emma Terry and has a calendar for 1975. Courtesy Meisinger Collection.

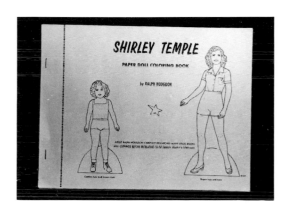

Shirley Temple Paper Doll Coloring Book done by Ralph Hodgdon in 1977. It contains 50 Shirley costumes, with many from movies. Very well done. Courtesy Meisinger Collection.

From Ralph Hodgdon's paper doll coloring book. Costumes by William Lambert. Courtesy Meisinger Collection.

Mini Series "original paper dolls" by Emma Terry. 1977. Courtesy Meisinger Collection.

Emma Terry used a Shirley Temple doll as her paper doll in this set with movie clothes. Courtesy Meisinger Collection.

English advertisement for Quaker Wheat and Quaker Rice. Courtesy Meisinger Collection.

Advertising for the Shirley Temple doll in the Toy World and Bicycle World. November 1934. Courtesy Meisinger Collection.

Art Photo (Great Britain) #36-2 Birthday card. Number on front is 11½V-5. Courtesy Meisinger Collection.

1976 Greeting Card by Dimensional
Services of Peoria, IL. Inside shows
names of people born on this date and
year. Courtesy Meisinger Collection.

Greeting card/note paper
made and designed by
LaVonne Johnston.
Courtesy Meisinger Collection.

Greeting card or note paper
that is new and may still be
available. Courtesy Meis-
inger Collection.

Note pads available from
Kay Bransky. Courtesy
Meisinger Collection.

Hard bound book "Film Stars of the World". Printed in England, it contains a great many sepia photos along with a short biography and list of films. Movie credits for Shirley go to *Rebecca of Sunnybrook Farm*. 1938. Courtesy Meisinger Collection.

Page 71 from the book "Film Stars of the World". Courtesy Meisinger Collection.

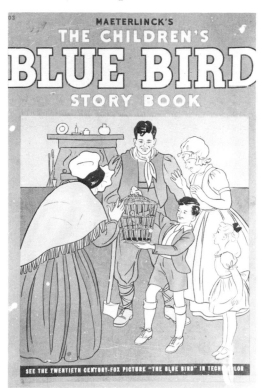

This story book Maeterlinck's The Children's Blue Bird Story Book was printed by Whitman Publishing Co. in 1940. The illustrations were by Sari. Courtesy Meisinger Collection.

Hard bound book "Film Pictorial Annual-1940" has Shirley on the cover in color and a few pictures inside. Printed in England. Courtesy Meisinger Collection.

Hard bound with dust jacket, "Shirley Temple" by Robert Windeler Published in 1976 in England. Courtesy Meisinger Collection.

From Robert Windeler's book "Shirley Temple" and shows Shirley Temple Black with her daughter. Courtesy Meisinger Collection.

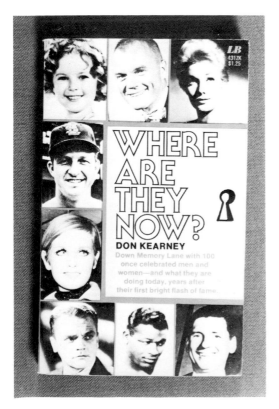

Paperback book "Where Are They Now" by Don Kearney. Published in 1977. Courtesy Meisinger Collection.

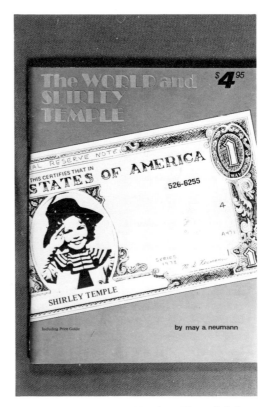

"The World and Shirley Temple" by May A. Neumann. This little book is currently available and contains many Shirley items and current prices. Courtesy Meisinger Collection.

"Shirley's Baby Book" by
Lorraine Burdick. This is
booklet #5 in her series.
Courtesy Meisinger Collection.

Shirley's Fashions and
Features, a booklet by Lorraine Burdick. Book #6 in a
series on Shirley Temple.
Courtesy Meisinger Collection.

A soft cover book by Lor-
raine Burdick. Many
beautiful photos. Courtesy
Meisinger Collection.

Shirley Temple in "de kleine
Prinses"-Little Princess.
This booklet is from Den-
mark. It describes the movie
and has over ten photos.
Courtesy Meisinger Collection.

"Alverdens Barnestjerner"
by Arnold Hending and
printed in Denmark. This
paperback book covers a
great many child stars and
was published in 1949.
Courtesy Meisinger Collection.

"Gracia y Simpatia". This is
a pulp type book of *Baby
Take A Bow* with a center
section of black and white
photos and produced by Ediciones Bistagne that also put
out many postcards. (Spain).
Booklet also contains ap-
plication to join the Shirley
Temple Club. Courtesy Meisinger Collection.

Booklet from the Victoria & Albert Museum, "Dolls" by Caroline Goodfellow and printed in England. Courtesy Meisinger Collection.

Book mark of heavy cardboard, from Spain. Courtesy Meisinger Collection.

This is the Dutch Club paper of about 1939. Features *The Little Princess* on the cover. Courtesy Meisinger Collection.

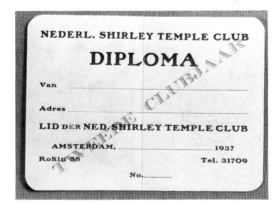

Diploma for the Shirley Temple Club in Amsterdam, Holland. 1937. Has photo of Shirley on front side. Courtesy Meisinger Collection.

The English publication "Film Pictorial" of September 22, 1934 featured Shirley on the cover. Courtesy Meisinger Collection.

The English publication "Film Pictorial" of December 20, 1934 featured Shirley on the cover. Courtesy Meisinger Collection.

"Mid-Week Pictorial" for May 19, 1934 with Shirley on the cover. Printed at Times Square, New York. Courtesy Meisinger Collection.

"Entertainment" Magazine of July 2, 1934. First United States cover (in black and white), also had story that compared Shirley Temple to a china doll. Courtesy Rita Dubas. Photo by John DeLuca.

"Gente Menuda" of December 1935. This is a child's booklet printed in Spain. Courtesy Meisinger Collection.

"Film Pictorial" of September 7, 1935 had Shirley on the cover. Courtesy Meisinger Collection.

Birthday issue of "Film Pictorial" (England) had a cover of Shirley Temple along with an article. April 25, 1936. Courtesy Meisinger Collection.

"Cinegrams", July 1935. Spanish Movie Magazine cover. Courtesy Rita Dubas. Photo by John DeLuca.

The British Magazine "Picturegoer" of
September 5, 1936 featured Shirley
on the cover and an article entitled
Poor Little Rich Girl. Courtesy Meisinger Collection.

"Movie Mirror" Album of Stars and
given with the compliments of the
J.J. Newberry Co. This is a very rare
item. The entire magazine is done in
green tones. Courtesy Meisinger Collection.

The April 3, 1937 issue of "Picturegoer" (England) featured Shirley
on the cover *Dimples.* Inside was a 16
page booklet with pictures and story
of *Dimples.* Courtesy Meisinger Collection.

"Filmjournalen" Magazine. Cover.
(Swedish). July 24, 1938. Courtesy
Rita Dubas. Photo by John DeLuca.

This page from "Sketch" Magazine is dated September 23, 1936. Courtesy Meisinger Collection.

Page from "Sketch" (England) of May 27, 1936. Courtesy Meisinger Collection.

A page from a Spanish magazine showing Shirley at Christmas. Courtesy Meisinger Collection.

A page from a Spanish magazine with photo of Shirley. Courtesy Meisinger Collection.

Another Spanish page from a magazine. Courtesy Meisinger Collection.

Shows Shirley from *Little Miss Broadway*. This is a page from a Spanish magazine. Courtesy Meisinger Collection.

July 31, 1937 issue of the "Film Weekly" featured a cover of Shirley Temple from *Stowaway* there is also a review of the film inside. Printed in London. Courtesy Meisinger Collection.

"West Coast Review of Books" has Shirley on the cover and photo of her with Walt Disney inside. 1975. Courtesy Meisinger Collection.

"TWA Ambassador" Magazine cover of 1976 has a cover of stars and it is easy to pick out Shirley Temple. Courtesy Meisinger Collection.

A Magazine of Social Sciences "Human Behavior" of December 1977 featured a cover with Shirley Temple and an article which includes her. Courtesy Meisinger Collection.

August 1, 1977 issue of "Film Collector's World" featured a center fold of photos as well as the cover to Shirley Temple. Courtesy Meisinger Collection.

The May 1977 magazine "Bestways" has an article about Gayelord Hauser, which includes a photo of Shirley Temple telling him she eats her spinach. Courtesy Meisinger Collection.

The magazine "Peninsula" (San Francisco) of February 1977 has a cover photo of Shirley Temple Black and an article. Courtesy Meisinger Collection.

The July 1977 issue of the "Wairarapa Doll News" from Australia featured a photo of Shirley on the cover and also has an article and knitting instruction for making outfits for a 16" vinyl Shirley doll.

April 22, 1978 issue of "Weekend Magazine" from Toronto, Ontario. Has excellent color photos and coverage of Shirley Temple from a child to her 50th birthday. Courtesy Meisinger Collection.

Connecticut Nutr

Published Every Thursday

NEW CANAAN, CONN., JUNE 2, 1938

Thanks, Shirley!

May 19, 1938

Dear Mr. Bye,

The Connecticut Nutmeg is a very nice name for a magazine. I hope you and your friends have a lot of success with it.

Love,

Shirley Temple

The "Connecticut Nutmeg" was published in New Canaan, Connecticut and this issue, which is Volume 1, No. 2 of June 2, 1938, carries a photo and letter wishing for success from Shirley Temple. This delightful little magazine was owned and edited by some pretty famous people, such as : Quentin Reynolds, Gene Tunney, George T. Bye, Deems Taylor and Ursula Parrot. One of the columns was called "Going Places" by Corneluis Vanderbilt, Jr. Courtesy Meisinger Collection.

Shirley Temple a Safety Ranger

Shirley Temple, outstanding screen star and loved by millions, has long been a member of the Lone Ranger's Safety Club. Shirley, although kept very busy with her acting and studies, does much to help promote safety in California, where she is a Safety Ranger. Shirley can now be seen in her latest picture Just Around the Corner.—Photograph through courtesy of Twentieth Century Fox.

Butter-Nut Bread Co. put out the publication, "Lone Ranger News" and this issue of December, 1936 carried the news that Shirley Temple was a Safety Ranger. This is Volume 1, No. 3. Published in Springfield, IL. Courtesy Meisinger Collection.

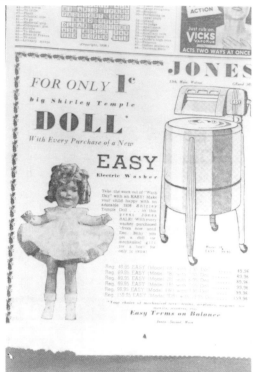

An interesting ad in a 1936 newspaper for a Shirley Temple doll. Says "Slightly soiled". Courtesy Alma Carmichael.

This ad in a 1936 newspaper shows that the doll will be given with a purchase. Courtesy Alma Carmichael.

This was a tiny ad in a 1936 newspaper. It shows the coloring set with Shirley's name on the front. Courtesy Alma Carmichael.

New York Sunday News Cover. October 15, 1944. Courtesy Rita Dubas. Photo by John DeLuca.

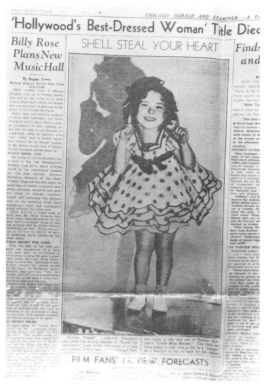

Chicago Herald Examiner of June 3, 1934 had photo of Shirley. Courtesy Meisinger Collection.

Des Moines Sunday Register featured this two full pages, life size photo of Shirley. Date was April 19, 1936. Shown with Shirley is one of the Dionne Quints. Courtesy Meisinger Collection.

Special Shirley Temple Edition of Yester-Year of February 1977. Courtesy Meisinger Collection.

Full size 27" x 40" poster for *That Hagen Girl*. 1947. Courtesy Meisinger Collection.

Shirley Temple Pressbook for *Little Miss Broadway*. These press books went out to the movie houses so they could chose the size and types of ad campaigns that they wanted to use to promote the picture. It also has ads for dolls and contests. Courtesy Meisinger Collection.

This page from the pressbook for *Little Miss Broadway* shows the many fan photos that were available to the movie house owners. Courtesy Meisinger Collection.

Page from pressbook of *Little Miss Broadway*. Contains promotional ideas such as transfers, props and contests. Courtesy Meisinger Collection.

This page from the pressbook of *Little Miss Broadway* shows many of the tie in items, such as clothing, ribbons, doll, etc. Courtesy Meisinger Collection.

19" x 16" black and white poster #1009 by Contemp Products Corp. Boston, Mass. 1971. Drawing is by Morello. Courtesy Meisinger Collection.

"Roxy Review" 1936. Shirley Temple on the cover and inside *Stowaway* to be next attraction. Courtesy Rita Dubas. Photo by John DeLuca.

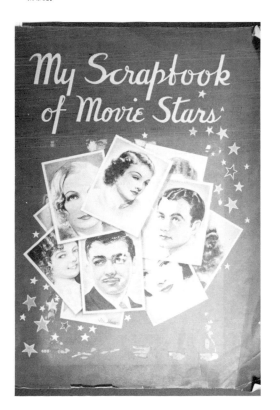

She Always Knows What to Do. Seldom does Shirley make a mistake during a scene. She learns the lines for her pictures at night, after she gets in bed. Most of her pictures are finished several days ahead of schedule. She usually finishes her day's work by 4 p. m.

"My Scrapbook of Movie Stars". This one follows Shirley's career through to the 1940's. The following seven photos are some of the items in this particular scrapbook. Courtesy Meisinger Collection.

"Curly Top." In this picture, released in 1935, Shirley depicted a 65-year-old woman. She is said to receive $50,000 a picture from the 20th Century-Fox studio under her latest contract. She has a large trust fund.

No Baby Talk. Shirley's mother, whom the star calls "Mom," reared her without baby talk, one reason Shirley's speech is so good and her singing so easy to understand.

Shirley and Her Parents. Mr. and Mrs. Temple realize the great responsibility they have in the most famous little girl in the world. They do all in their power to keep her happy. Despite her fame and fortune, she leads a normal, healthy life. Her big brothers treat her just as a baby sister, not as a movie star. Her father often bathes her. Sometimes she wears sunbonnets.

Her Name Is Magic. This is another scene from "Curly Top," with Shirley as a bride. She gets more from "Shirley Temple" products than from acting, probably receives a half million dollars a year, and turns even more away.

AGE SEVEN. Shirley was a real trouper by 1936 and "Stowaway" (above) did much to make her Hollywood's biggest box-office attraction

Kidding Hollywood. The "baby burlesques" made fun of the movies and movie stars. Here Shirley imitates a widely known actress. Since those days her parents have rejected huge offers made to Shirley for radio and personal appearances. They want to keep her unspoiled

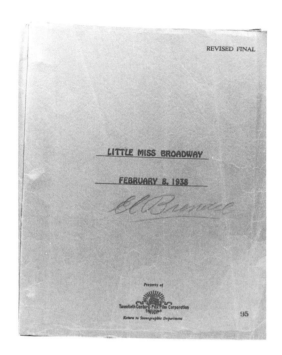

Script for *Little Miss Broadway*. Approved February 8, 1938. This copy belonged to El Brendel who played "Ole", the vaudevillian in the film. Script No. 95. Red binder. Courtesy Rita Dubas. Photo by John DeLuca.

Seein' Stars Stamp #49 in series. Courtesy Meisinger Collection.

Academy of Motion Picture Arts and Sciences movie photo stamps. Printed in 1941. The stamp with Shirley says "Special Award 1934 for outstanding contribution to motion pictures." Courtesy Meisinger Collection.

Spanish ad for LaRambla Cinema for the movie *I'll Be Seeing You* 1943-44, although ad is dated 1946. The Spanish title is *I'll See You Again*. Translation courtesy Chris Paez. Courtesy Meisinger Collection.

French advertisement for Hotel a
Vendre-*Little Miss Broadway*.
Courtesy Meisinger Collection.

These 1930's valentines were not sold
as Shirley Temple items, but the
Shirley influence can be seen.
Courtesy Meisinger Collection.

"Doll" wrapping paper made and designed by LaVaughn Johnston. Courtesy Meisinger Collection.

Card sent to fan requesting a photo. The envelope has a $.01 stamp imprint. Photo on other side of card is Shirley standing by a chair and is signed "Love Shirley Temple". Courtesy Meisinger Collection.

1935 candid shot taken by a fan of Shirley in Hawaii. Courtesy Meisinger Collection.

Candid snap shot by a fan of Shirley in Hawaii. Courtesy Meisinger Collection.

1977 autographed photo of Shirley Temple Black when she was Chief of Protocol. Courtesy Meisinger Collection.

Photo autographed by Shirly Temple Black in 1977. Courtesy Meisinger Collection.

A give-a-way photo from Australia. Courtesy Meisinger Collection.

Smiling Shirley Temple photo presented with Women's Companion (British). Courtesy Meisinger Collection.

This is a movie still 8 x 10 glossy with a profile shot of Shirley Temple. Courtesy Meisinger Collection.

These are some photos that have been cut from something. They have photos on each side. Good quality paper and may have been proofs. All are sepia tone. Courtesy Meisinger Collection.

This page shows the same photos that have been cut from something. There are photos on each side of the pages. Courtesy Meisinger Collection.

German-Dutch publicity photo on heavy cardboard. Glossy is marked Ross Verlag. May have been part of a calendar. 5" x 7" 1930's. Courtesy Rita Dubas. Photo by John DeLuca.

Large 11" x 14" sepia photo. This photo was used in postcards, interviews, etc. Courtesy Meisinger Collection.

Shows two new decks of playing cards. No maker information is on the cards. Courtesy Meisinger Collection.

Three very good quality Spanish cards with gold band around edge. Date unknown. Courtesy Meisinger Collection.

November 10, 1934. Popular Song Hits put out by Engel-Van Wiseman, Inc. Courtesy Meisinger Collection.

Phonograph record that is more than 1/8" thick. The recording is only on one side. Title: Sing Me An Old Fashioned Love Song. Artist: Shirley Temple & Vocal Ensemble. Picture: *Little Miss Broadway*. 6646-Recording's Incorporated-Hollywood. The other side is engraved: Allied Phonograph & Record Mfg. This is the "master" record from which other records were duplicated. Courtesy Thelma Kimble.

British song sheet "Together". Copyright 1944. Printed by Campbell, Connelly & Co. London. Courtesy Meisinger Collection.

Springboard International's record of 1977, "The Best of Shirley Temple". Courtesy Meisinger Collection.

HRB Music Co. record "The Best of Shirley Temple". 1978. Courtesy Meisinger Collection.

Simplicity pattern #2717 with outfits for the 12" Shirley Temple doll. 1958. Courtesy Meisinger Collection.

Dress and pattern by American Thread Co. Leaflet #45, November 1935. Courtesy Meisinger Collection.

Pattern of 1942 by "Hollywood" for
20" "Star Dolls". Pattern number is
1913. Courtesy Meisinger Collection.

Left is card #404 in the series from
the movie house Cine Miria in Spain.
The other is to show an example of the
backs of these cards. Courtesy Meisinger Collection.

Three trade cards from movie houses
in Spain. Left to right: Cine America,
Cine Miria and Cine Barcelona.
Courtesy Meisinger Collection.

These two Spanish trade cards are from the movie houses of: Left: Cine America and right: Pathe Palace. Courtesy Meisinger Collection.

Left to right: Marked "Ross". Center one is marked Paramount and is #78 in Film Stars Series and issued by John Sinclair Ltd. Newcastle-on-tyne. (England). Last one is also marked "Ross". The Ross cards are from Holland. Courtesy Meisinger Collection.

Left is a Trade Card from Holland, marked "Ross" and the other is #1 in John Sinclair Ltd. (England) Film Star Series. Courtesy Meisinger Collection.

Metal Bank and a current item. Courtesy Meisinger Collection.

Very deep box. May have been used as a gift box, candy box or for cards and stationary. Blue on white photo. Trim. No mark. 1930's. Courtesy Rita Dubas. Photo by John DeLuca.

Designer Series belt buckle by Oden. Courtesy Meisinger Collection.

Current shower curtain/window curtains that contains many scenes from movies including several poses of Shirley Temple. Courtesy Meisinger Collection.

Safety Star Film from Montgomery
Wards. Contains 50 feet of film titled
"Shirley Temple-The Wonder Child".
Courtesy Meisinger Collection.

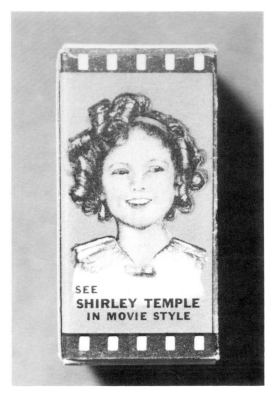

Shows the side of one of the boxes of
films made by Allied Mfg. Co.
Courtesy Meisinger Collection.

Allied Mfg. Co. film set 1 through 12
of Shirley Temple in movie scenes.
Courtesy Meisinger Collection.

Child's Party Favor Puzzle. Glass covered with two marbles. Marked: Made in Japan. 2" diameter. 1930's. Courtesy Rita Dubas. Photo by John DeLuca.

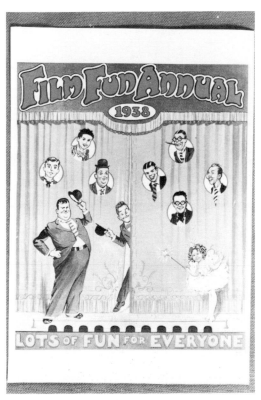

1976 I.P.C. Card Juvenile Division of Chimera Arts, London titled "Film Fun Annual" 1938. Courtesy Meisinger Collection

6" Tall Thermo-type mug purchased recently and made by Flambeau. Also has miniature lobby stills of *Tarzan and the Leopard Woman* and Mary Pickford in *Rebecca of Sunnybrook Farm*. Courtesy Meisinger Collection.

Current T-shirt with impressed/hot iron on photo of Shirley Temple. Courtesy Meisinger Collection.

117

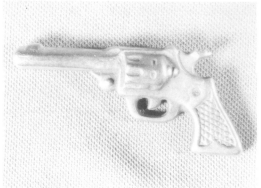

This is the close up of the gun that came in the holster of the mint Ranger (Cowgirl) doll owned by Alma Carmichael. The doll can be seen in the color section.

Postcard marked: Ross Verlag. Courtesy Rita Dubas. Photo by John DeLuca.

Three U.S. publicity postcards sent to fan's requests. All sepia. Left to right: 1937 20th Fox, 1938 20th Fox, and 1941 MGM. Courtesy Rita Dubas. Photo by John DeLuca.

The two top cards are unmarked. The lower left is from France and the lower right is from a Spanish series B and #4. Courtesy Meisinger Collection.

Left: FS 6 and right: C 289 Colourgraph Series, 85 Long Acre, London. Courtesy Meisinger Collection.

Upper: FS 17, lower: FS 43, 85 Long Acre, London. Courtesy Meisinger Collection.

Left: FS10 and right: FS9, 85 Long Acre, London. Courtesy Meisinger Collection.

Left: FS48, right: FS45. 85 Long Acre, London. Courtesy Meisinger Collection.

Upper: FS50, lower: FS 65, 85 Long Acre, London. Courtesy Meisinger Collection.

Upper: FS86 and lower: FS157. 85 Long Acre, London. Courtesy Meisinger Collection.

Upper: F.S.114 and lower: FS 87. 85 Long Acre, London. Courtesy Meisinger Collection.

Upper: FS77 and lower: FS 67, 85 Long Acre, London. Courtesy Meisinger Collection.

Left: FS68 and right: FS83, 85 Long Acre, London. Courtesy Meisinger Collection.

Left: #FS 156 and right: #FS 111, 85 Long Acre, London. Courtesy Meisinger Collection.

Upper: FS 167 and lower: FS 171, 85 Long Acre, London. Courtesy Meisinger Collection.

None of these cards have any identifying marks or numbers. They are a pulp-type paper and yellow with age. Most likely from England. Courtesy Meisinger Collection.

All three, (except the upper right) are the yellowed, pulp-type cards, maybe from England. The upper right is a postcard and also a trade card and is #42 in series by DE RESZKE Cigarettes and other Godfrey Phillips brands. Courtesy Meisinger Collection.

Four more of the pulp-type cards that have no marks and may be from England. Courtesy Meisinger Collection.

These cards are unmarked, are of the pulp-type paper, yellow with age and most likely from England. Courtesy Meisinger Collection.

These four post cards are only marked with "infonal" on the back and no other information. Courtesy Meisinger Collection.

Two English postcards from 85 Long Acre, London. Right is #FS 181 and left is FS 174. Courtesy Meisinger Collection.

Upper: #FS183 in the English series with only maker's identity on card: 85 Long Acre, London. Lower: #FS 184 in same series. Courtesy Meisinger Collection.

Both these post cards are marked 85 Long Acre, London and the upper is #FS 203 and the lower: #FS 186. Courtesy Meisinger Collection.

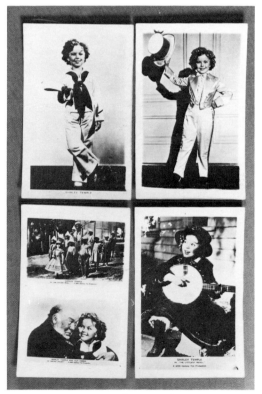

Left is No. C 409 Colorgraph Series, 85 Long Acre, London. Right is #P1143 Show Parade Picture Service, 128 Long Acre, London. Courtesy Meisinger Collection.

All four cards are from Italy. Courtesy Meisinger Collection.

Left is an unmarked card and right:
B-41 British Production. Courtesy
Meisinger Collection.

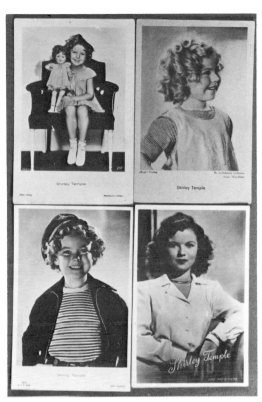

Two upper cards are "Ross" Verlag
(Holland) and lower left is Italy mark-
ed: 3516 B.F.F.Edit. Lower right is
#3027 and from Holland. Courtesy
Meisinger Collection.

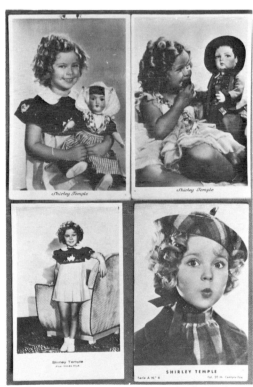

The upper two are marked: Echte
Photographie. Lower left is from Italy
and lower right is unmarked except
for Series A No. 6. Courtesy Meisinger
Collection.

The upper card is from Italy and the
lower one from the Netherlands.
Courtesy Meisinger Collection.

Series #1 and 2 of unknown series of cards. May be from Spain. Courtesy Meisinger Collection.

Ediciones Bistagne (Spain) series #3, 2 & lower, #5 and 4. Courtesy Meisinger Collection.

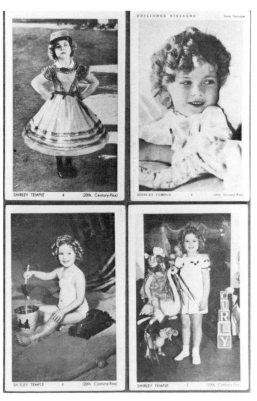

Both these cards are from one set and only marked: Fuera de serie. Courtesy Meisinger Collection.

All but upper right are from one Spanish series and are #6, 5 & 4. Other is #6 in set from Ediciones Bistagne. Courtesy Meisinger Collection.

All but upper right are from a Spanish series and are #1, 3 & 2. Upper right is #6 in Ediciones Bistagne set. Courtesy Meisinger Collection.

Upper left, #3, right #1. Lower left #5 and lower right is #4 in the Ediciones Bistagne series. (Spain). Courtesy Meisinger Collection.

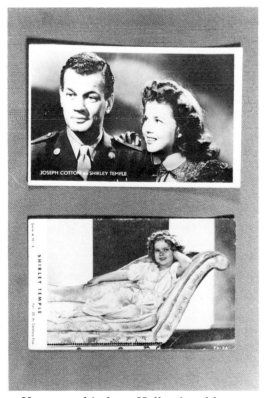

Upper left, unmarked. Right: from Vanguard Studio. Lower left from Holland and lower right Series 1, also from Holland. Courtesy Meisinger Collection.

Upper card is from Holland and lower one unmarked but for #TU-36 and Serie A No. 4. Courtesy Meisinger Collection.

Left is from Holland and right is from a series #96 and from Spain. Courtesy Meisinger Collection.

Upper card is from the Netherlands and the lower card is unmarked. Courtesy Meisinger Collection.

Left is marked Argenta and right is from the Netherlands. Courtesy Meisinger Collection.

Left: from Italy and the right one is from Holland and marked "Ross" Verlag. Courtesy Meisinger Collection.

All four cards are from Holland and marked with "Ross" Verlag. Courtesy Meisinger Collection.

Additions To Bibliography

Additions To Bibliography (Con't.)

Sketch, The (British) . . . . . 8-1-34 (P&A), 5-27-36 (P)
9-16-36 (P), 9-23-36 (P), 12-30-36 (P&A), 1-4-39
(P&A), 11-16-38 (P), 2-15-39 (P)
Societe Parisienne D'Edition (French) . . . 11-12-52 (P)
Song Parade . . . . 7-44 (P)
Star . . . . 1-25-77 (P)
St. Nicholas Mag. . . . . 10-36 (P), 11-36 (P), 4-37, 6-37
Super Puzzler of the Movies . . . . Winter 1976 (P)
Time . . . . 11-1-76 (P)
Toy World . . . . 11-34 (P)
True Movie & Television . . . . 8-50 (A)
True Love & Romance 2-45

True Romances . . . . 4-45 (P)
True Story . . . . 4-38 (P), 7-47, 9-47, 6-48
TWA Ambassador . . . . 4-76 (C)
Whisper . . . . 4-56 (P)
Who's Who of Hollywood . . . . 1961 (P&A)
Western Family . . . . 11-20-41 (C&A)
US . . . . 5-2-78 Family Album (P&A)
Yesteryear . . . . 2-77 (Shirley Temple Issue), 4-77
Nov. 1978 (Shirley Temple Issue)
Young Miss . . . . 1-74 (P)
Your Future For 1939 . . . . (P)
Your Story in the Stars by Wynn . . . . 1934 (P)

Books

All Americans, The, 1977, J.R. Parish & D. Stanke
Alverdens Barnestjerner by Arnold Hending, 1949
(Denmark)
Encyclopedia Brittanica Yearbook, 1959 (P)
Film Daily 20th Anniversary No. 1938 (P)
Film Lovers Annual, (British) 1934 (P)
Film Pictorial Annual, (British) 1938 (P), 1939 (P&A)
Films of Shirley Temple 1978, Robert Windeler
Film Stars of the World, 1937 (British) (P)
Film Stars-Who's Who of the Screen, 1936 (C), 1939
(C)
Good Old Days, David Cohn, 1940
Gracia y Simpatia (Spain) Baby Take A Bow 5-20-36
Hamlyn History of the Movies, Mary Davies, Janice
Anderson & Peter Arnold. (British) 1975 (P)
Hollywood Album, (N.Y. Times) 1977 (P)

Hollywood Character Actors, J.R. Parish 1978 (P)
Hollywood Costume Design, 1976
I Like America, 1939 (BR.), Geoffrey Harmsworth
Introducing the Song Sheet, Helen Westin, Thomas
Nelson, Inc. 1976 (C&A)
Memory Book of Great Movie Music, 1976 (P)
Modern Collector Dolls IV, 1978, Patricia R. Smith
Picture Show Film Star Album (British)
Secrets of the Stars, Denis Myers (British) 1950
Star Shots, John Engstead, 1978 (P)
Superstars, 1978 (British), Alexander Walker
Twentieth Century Dolls, Vol. I & II, Johana Anderton
TV Guide, The First 25 Years, 1978, Jay S. Harris
The Thirties, Alan Jenkins 1976
World and Shirley Temple, The, May Neuman 1978
World Book Annual, 1949